I Wish I Never...

While RVing

Sue Sadler

Illustrated by John Rose

Printed by Inside the Slides, LLC. www.insidetheslides.com
ISBN: 978-1-7332168-0-7 (paperback)

978-1-7332168-1-4 (ebook)

FIRST EDITION, VOLUME 1

This is a work of fiction and nonfiction. Names, characters, places, and incidents are the product of the author's imagination or creativity or are used in varying degrees of accuracy. Any resemblance to actual persons, living or dead, events or locales is entirely coincidental.

Disclaimer: Once upon a time.... no, One day, scratch that, One time while...

The stories in this book are real, the names have been changed to protect the innocent guilty and for those who have just YET to make these same mistakes. *Look for the humor in our mistakes, don't take them too seriously and yes, we love to RV!* We would never consider stopping. Nothing in this book should be taken as absolute fact and the graphics are to be a fun depiction of the intent, not accurate portrayal of the story.

As I traveled across this beautiful country, I quickly came to realize we all had stories about the mishaps of this great thing known as RVing. Whether it happened to us, we saw it happen or we just heard the stories, it's the story of a true family experience while Rving.

Sit back and enjoy the stories as told by the actual people who suffered the calamity or, for some of us, calamities! If you are part of the calamity club feel free to join us on our Facebook page at "I wish I never." Misery does love company!

Try not to repeat our errors and enjoy the open roads, mountains and streams. Hope to see you along the way. Happy Trails!

Table of Contents

About the Author

I started on this adventure as a girl tent camping under the stars. It was a love of those late-night fire circles, you know those glowing embers as they dwindle down towards sleep time? I would imagine them as the lights of a great city just showing off. Growing up in a small town, every- thing seemed like the "big city."

Over the years, not loving the tent floors any longer, I graduated to a cot, but still loved the quiet of the late-night fire pit after getting the kids off to bed. After 10 moves in 20 years, I landed in Reno, Nevada. The mountains and lakes were a huge draw to many campers. All around were these amazing travel trailers and motorhomes. What the heck, I'm in.

In 2006, I started my RVing with "hard sides" in a class C oldie of 1984 vintage. Grew up into a 1986 Class A which served me well on many an adventure; not much to look at but it all worked. As I neared retirement age, I dreamed of owning one of the big ones, the shiny ones I saw running down the highway. In 2016 that became my reality. A 43' Class A motorhome ready to be my last motorhome, as I call it. It has led me to full time RVing across the USA.

Enjoy the stories of many fellow RVers as we tell everything "I WISH I NEVER ...."

Pulled the Release

When you believe that you have found the perfect location in your camping spot to stop, drop and roll? Joe and Tomi from West Palm Beach, Florida are traveling west. "Go West," as the saying goes. Both were excited to be stopping for the night in the perfect little campground in the Black Hills of South Dakota. Beautiful trees, green grass and a welcoming host were the icing on the cake as they checked in at the front desk. Now map in hand, they are off to their camp site.

Being a pull-through space, they quickly located their number and pulled their 5th wheel camper forward into what would be their long gravel, gently sloped home away from home for a few weeks.

Joe pulled to a stop, ensuring his connections were all within reach. Satisfied that everything was just right, he pulled the release on the 5th wheel camper and pulled forward to hear BAM! I wish I never....

I wish I never... *pulled the release for my 5th wheel camper trailer to disconnect from the truck BEFORE I put the jacks down.*

Two huge dents in truck bed, damage the entire front of the 5th wheel camper leaving a hole in it. REPAIRS: $7,250.00

Pulled Into the Drive-Thru

Fresh air always brings out the best in appetites while on the road. After a long day of driving, Cynthia decided it was time for a quick bite. Finding the perfect exit with several options, she headed for the "burger joint" with a drive-thru.

"Augh," she said to herself, the line is so long. "Why can't I get hungry at a less busy time?" As she slowly approached the front of the line to order, there was a THUD! What?

Oh no! As she stuck her head out the window and looked up, she could see that the top of her trailer was NOT going to fit under the drive-thru awning. Now, normally that wouldn't be all that bad. She could just back up and park, go inside and finally get that dinner, but .... There were 10 vehicles in line behind her.

I wish I never... *pulled into a drive-thru with 10 cars behind me only to figure out I won't fit under the awning.*

Small dented line across the trailer where the canopy hit, humiliation and a few heated comments thrown at her. REPAIRS: dent removed and touch up paint. $1245.00, humiliation...enormous.

Hose Still Connected

When you believe that campgrounds need watering and you are just the right person to do it. Bob and Sandy had just packed up their motor- home. Sandy is doing her normal activities, closing the inside so nothing falls or tumbles while going down the road. Bob is working on shutting up everything on the exterior.

Along comes the camp ground host, Jerry to thank them for staying and asks Bob if he'd mind helping put the picnic table back up on the site. They move the picnic table and make chit chat. Sandy yells out, "all set", let's do it. Bob looks left to right and all looks ready to go.

They hop in ready to head for home. As they pull out of the space and near the exit they hear shouts from others screaming for them to stop! A quick glance back at the recently abandoned camping spot reveals a fountain that was not there before they pulled out. I wish I never ....

I wish I never... *pulled out of the campground with the water hose still connected to the water spigot.*

Breaking out our water connection on the motorhome, pulling the water pipe out of the ground and flooding the camping area. REPAIRS: $1,500.00 in expenses.

A Tire Blow Out

Tom was heading to a popular race track to spend the weekend enjoying the life of fast cars, looking forward to meeting his buddies for some much-needed rest and relaxation. Unfortunately, getting his work done took longer than expected. He ended up leaving a little later than planned from work, so he had to take a few short cuts in the pre-check to make up some time.

Driving down the highway with the music jamming, he heard an insane BOOM, BANG, CRASH. His trailer was weaving heavily from left to right. He immediately slowed the rig to the right side of the highway. As he exited the truck he could see pieces and parts of his tire on the 5th wheel shredded along the road behind him.

After calling for roadside assistance, he went inside the camper to wait. OH MY GOSH...he screams as he sees that the tire had blown up through the wheel well, through a cabinet and into the camper. I wish I never ....

I wish I never... *learned how damaging a tire blowing can be on my rig. Check tires every trip!*

Tire blew up through the floor of 5th wheel, required replacement of cabinets, flooring and wheel well. REPAIRS: $4,820.

Power Still Connected

Some places you visit are just breathtaking. RV adventures allowing travel to faraway places and the sightseeing at the wonders of this great country are never ending.

Family adventures leave lasting memories for everyone. The Jenkins from Zanesville, Ohio took off to visit the Blue Ridge Mountains. Mom, Dad with their 5 children ages 2 to 10 in their camper ready for nature, hiking, camp fires and some needed downtime. In July, we all know how crowded the parks can be, but they planned and booked a great camp- ground with lots of amenities for everyone to enjoy. After two weeks of fun it was time to head home.

Plans were to stop in the Hocking Hills of Southern Ohio on the way back home for a lastbreather.

Pulling out of the campground, well-rested and ready for the next stop they saw people yelling at them to STOP! I wish I never ....

I wish I never... *pulled out of our camp site with the power still connected to thepedestal...*

Ripped the pedestal right out of the frame with power cord still attached. REPAIRS: Electrical repairs to campground site, new pedestal and electrician's labor:
$1,108.00. Canceling going to Hocking Hills... disappointing.

Crossed Railroad Tracks

Getting out and enjoying the outdoors is what David and Nicole love most to do in their free time. They are proud of the fact that they can get out and go on the weekends to new places.

As they traveled along the country side in the Midwest in their RV, they marveled at the small towns and the simple way of life. Stopping along the way to do some shopping and stop at a sidewalk café for lunch, life was good.

Heading to their campground for the night, they looked at the map and found a nice backroad shortcut that would get them to the camp nearly an hour sooner. "Sweet," said Nicole, "we can enjoy the sunset." They agreed it would be fun to take the backroad and off they went.

As they approached the railroad crossing, all seemed well. A second later, SCREECHING and SCRAPING and then an instant STOP! "Oh no!" yells David, "we are stuck!" I wish I never....

I wish I never... *went across steep up and down railroad tracks and bottomed out my motorhome across them!*

Tow truck to lift the front of the motorhome up and drag the back up and over the tracks; dents along the cargo holds, which were left as a reminder; shutting down road and railroad for 6 hours: REPAIRS: $700.00 for tow truck and 6 hours of embarrassment, dirty looks and aggravation.

Left the Satellite Dish

We loved the movie "UP" with the balloon that lifted an entire house with people in it across the countryside. What a marvel! It would seem like a cool idea if you could take your brick and mortar house and just take off to a new location whenever you felt like it. Right?

Well, on one recent trip we thought that that was exactly what we were doing with our motorhome. We packed up like normal and headed off to our next city of adventure, but while driving it felt like we were sailing. The motorhome just wouldn't stay in our lane, drifting left and right.

Everything that could be wrong started to cross your mind. Tires, engine, you name it! Luckily, we pulled over to find our problem which was literally acting like a sail on top of our rig. Yikes! I wish I never ....

I wish I never... *left the satellite dish up when driving 65 mph down the highway...*

Bent the satellite dish brackets and had to manually force it to go back down on top of the motorhome; REPAIRS: Replacing satellite dish mounting hardware $399.95 and a night in a hotel: $129.00, no roof damage...amazing.

Pulled Down Power Lines

Do you have one of those people who is always in a hurry? Wants to get going? Likes shortcuts? Well this story if for you and them.

While recently traveling toward Santa Fe, NM, Jake and Jennie were ready to find a stop for a couple of nights and check out the area. With no advance reservation they found a small RV park on the outskirts of town. Nice place, albeit a little older and smaller park than normal, but they gladly took the offer to stay for two nights.

Now if you haven't spent time in Santa Fe, it's not to be missed. The his- tory and art are amazing. After a day of galleries and museums Jake was ready to hit it. You know, get moving to their next adventure. Jennie, agreeable as always, packed up and they were ready to head out. Jake notices there's no one in the camp spot in front of them and a shortcut across that space would save time and take him straight to the exit rather than having to make several tight turns on the campground roads to get to the exit from the park. I wish I never ....

I wish I never... *went across a vacant camp spot to detour across to the exit and pull down the power lines with the top of my motorhome satellite.*

Had to call power company to remove power lines from motorhome and repair lines. REPAIRS: $750.00 for an emergency service call and re- pairs. Left campground without power for 4 hours.

Low Bridge Clearance

Ahhhh the fun of summer road construction puts even the best of us in a tizzy. Construction signs, reduced speeds, accidents that make it even worse, make some of us re-think taking to the highways for travels.

There's a favorite book that gives the most scenic routes to drive, pointing out interesting sights along the way. Derek and Mandy are fulltime RVers who received the book as a gift. Having to travel in the construction jungle time of year, they decided to use the back roads and see small towns and simpler sights traveling across the Midwest. The beautiful rivers, towns and quaint little restaurants made this a great decision.

As they moved along in their journey, they saw some local road construction up ahead. Watchful as ever, Derek looked at the clearance sign that read 13' 2". No problem. He knew they were only 12' 4 in height. After pulling slowly under the bridge, CRUNCH! I wish I never ....

I wish I never... *underestimated the amount of additional pavement added under an old bridge when the clearance sign never changed to reflect the lowerclearance.*

Totaled the 5th wheel camper, tearing open the entire front apron, demolishing the kitchen and all appliances. REPAIRS: $5,000.00 deductible; cancelled insurance; $54,734.00 replacement; and 2 weeks hotel $2,640.00. Blocked the road for 4 hours.

Left Our Suitcases

For some people the motorhome is a few wonderful weeks a year of bliss. Getting away from all the work, commitments and responsibilities to just sit and relax.

Patrick and Cindy, from Minneapolis, MN, both worked high stress Corporate America jobs and each year looked forward to a few getaways in their RV. This year it was to the beautiful New Jersey shore with a few other camping friends.

All they could think about for weeks was the sun and sand, sipping cold drinks and the water's edge rushing over their toes.

They packed all the usual: bathing suits, shorts, flip flops and threw in the beach must haves, like snorkel, fins and balls. Then, like all of us, Cindy realized she'd forgotten sunscreen and rushed to pick some up. Upon return she saw Patrick loaded up and ready. He yelled, "Let's go!" She jumped in the motorhome and off they went.

About 150 miles into the trip, Cindy asked "You did remember the beach stuff, right? asked Patrick. OH NO! I wish I never ....

I wish I never... *left our suitcases, beach stuff and the CAT at the front door and drove 150 miles before missing them.*

Turn around and back to the house. Adding 5 hours to the trip. REPAIRS: $110.00 in fuel, no repairs required.

Drove Off with the Jacks Not Up

"We love to camp!" said Betsy as she shared her trips with her friend Carl. "The funny part is we don't mind telling people we want to do it on the cheap!" chuckles Carl.

As they both retired and took off for the great outdoors, they relied on friends, family and boondocking for free places to camp. For nearly three years they have been successful in spending less than $1,000 on camping sites a year as full-timers.

"Now, boondocking is not without its moments of compromise," explained Carl. "We were excited when we were invited to stay at our friend's home in Atlanta for a month. The only issue was they were re-sodding the yard next to where we had to park.

We enjoyed 4 weeks visiting with them. When packing up to leave we now needed to gently traverse the new sodded area. While crossing going slow would have been no big deal.... except - I wish I never ....

I wish I never... *drove off with the jacks not up all the way while crossing my friends newly sodded lawn!*

Dug up a section about 12' wide by 30' long, 6" ruts, dug up their sprinklers. REPAIRS: $2,160.00 in re-sodding, soil work and repairs to sprinklers.

Focused On My Husband's Directions

If you have been traveling with an RV for long you know that there are sometimes tight spots you can get into. Not what you set out to find, but somehow, they find you.

On one of those day Butch and LaDonna were heading to visit some friends they hadn't seen in years. It was a little off the beaten path, so they took their time with the directions. As they arrived at the address it was a long country road with a mix of gravel and dirt for the last ¼ mile. Not concerned they turned down the drive and headed to their friend's home. Just before the home was a narrow opening in the fence. Butch jumps out and says, "I will direct you, just watch me and we will fit just fine." As LaDonna slowing pulls through the gate watching Butch's direction she hears CRUNCH! I wish I never ....

I wish I never... *focused on my husband's directions and disregarded my side of the motorhome hitting a fence.*

REPAIRS: Front corner and scrapped paint down the side of the motor- home. Body shop and paint repairs $9,834.00.

Let My Dog Run Free

When Jacob decided to go fulltime RVing, it had taken him a while to get his life together in the right direction. He was a single guy with his trusty dog, Bud. Now Bud was not a little thing by any means and it seemed that he certainly made up most of the rules for Bob and his existence.

When Jacob finally settled on a rig for him and Bud's grand adventure, it was a 2000 Sahara Safari 33' Class A Motorhome. It was just perfect for the two of them and their adventures across the miles.

One day while Jacob and Bud were about 3 hours into a weeklong trip to enjoy the mountains, they pulled into a fuel station to fill up. Jacob took Bud for his quick bathroom break and then back in the motorhome he went. "Such a good dog!"

While fueling Jacob pulled out the ladder to do the windshield washing and chuckled at Bud sitting in the driver's seat. Suddenly Bud jumped up and put his front feet on the air brake releasing it. I wish I never....

I wish I never... *let my dog run free in my motorhome while fueling. He released the brakes and the motorhome started rolling.*

A slight concussion, banged up arms and legs and Jacob found he just fit under his motorhome. REPAIRS: $3,846.00 slight damage to motor- home, a new ladder & ambulance and medical bills, also the repair costs when it hit the car in front of us costing another $949.00.

Opened the Motorhome Door While Driving

Well, I must say, this story hits close to home. It hits me right smack in the face. I am the culprit in this story.

Picking up our new motorhome with 6 hours of orientation and lots of notes on how-to do this and that, we were off. Heading back across the country from Florida to Nevada we would get lots of time to test out all the new features of this beauty. Excited and nervous, we headed up interstate 75 out of Florida. A few miles down the highway, while cruising along at 70 mph, I'm in the passenger seat. I can hear air whistling from the front entry door and it seems we didn't shut it tight.

As most of us have done may times in a car, I opened the door to slam it shut. Now as the door is nearly ripping out of my hand, I'm screaming, "PULL OVER!, PULL OVER!" with my feet now locked against the door frame and arms locked on the door handle to keep it from flying open and throwing me out of the motorhome, I was certain I was going to be thrown to my death and the door ripped off the motorhome. I kept screaming until we stopped. I wish I never ....

I wish I never... *opened the motorhome door while my husband drove 70 mph down the freeway...*

Nightmares of being sucked out the door, thrown to my death and the motorhome door going with me. REPAIRS: Near death experience and at least one year of life off my expected lifespan and a lesson gained.

Drove Off Without the Trailer

"Buying a camper is F-R-E-E-D-O-M," shouts Drew. "It gives me a quick getaway on weekends and vacation days when I can get them." After shopping or a while to find the perfect camper, he purchased a 14' travel trailer that he could easily pull with his truck around the Western states.

A three-day weekend is coming up, so he made plans to head out to the lake for some much-needed rest and relaxation. Keeping the camper stocked with essentials is key to a quick get in and go. A stop along the way for some groceries and beverages is a typical activity on all trips.

As the weekend approached, all was ready to go. H backed up to his trailer to hook up and head out when his phone rang. It was his mother, who doesn't call often, so he decided to take the call. As he went inside for his duffle bag they chatted away. He told her about the weekend plans and she was glad to hear he was off to relax and they said their goodbyes. Drew jumped in the truck and off he went. As he turned the first corner he looked in his mirror. I wish I never...

I wish I never... *drove off without hooking up my trailer to my truck...*

"No loss, just a DUH" Drew thought, "how could I be so dumb?" Back to hook up and then off for the long weekend. REPAIRS: Confirmed that some rest and relaxation are due.

Forgot to Close the Sewer Tank Valve

"Do you have any idea how hard it is to camp with my wife and 3 girls?" asks Trenton.

Not only is he the lone man in the rig, the girls have lots of stuff and always outnumber him. But as most dads would say, he loves every minute of it.

The girls range in age from 12 to 17 and he feels blessed that he and his wife Becky can get them to still enjoy time away as a family camping. It's been nearly 20 years since he and Becky bought their first travel trailer and have since upgraded to a motorhome as, over the years as the family grew. Remember the stuff that comes with more girls needs more space.

On a trip to the Carolinas, they enjoyed lots of sun, surf and sand. Like all things, eventually it was time to pack up and head out. As Trenton went to dump the tanks, coil hoses and the like, he realized the black tank was not draining. He opened and closed the valve a few times, flushed the toilet several times and still nothing. He decided to put on the backflush valve to hopefully loosen up what he was sure was too much toilet paper in the pipe. As he disconnected the sewer hose to install the backflush hose connection he forgot to close the valve. I wish I never ....

I wish I never... *forgot to close the value on my sewer tank when re- moving the sewer hose as it let loose and spewed gallons of raw sew- age onto me and the campground.*

Could not close the valve as it was full of toilet paper as it dumped gallons of sewage onto the campground. Of course, the campground saw it and it became a hazmat site. REPAIRS: $500.00 fine, 4 hours cleaning up the site and needed shower.

Put DEF in the Fuel Tank

We've learned over the years that patience is a virtue. Especially when it comes to camping. Driving, maintaining, general set-up and tear-down all can lead to headaches if you aren't careful. "Don't get us wrong, we love to camp and cannot imagine a life without our camper and the memories we have made," said Christy.

"My husband Treavor is the rock of the family. He's the one who keeps it all together and makes sure that when things go wrong he calmly guides us to the resolution. Me? I'm more of the storm in the storm. I can throw out some word bombs when things don't go my way."

One trip my husband became ill with the flu, so I was the captain of the 5th wheel and truck driving us home. We needed DEF, so I pulled into the truck stop. Treavor asked if I needed help and I told him I was fine to pump DEF and top off our fuel. Big mistake! I wish I never ....

I wish I never... *Put DEF in the truck's fuel tank instead of its own tank! My husband realized what I was doing and lost it. Waving, yelling and running towards me to stop!*

REPAIRS: Had to be towed out of the truck lane into a diesel shop. Tanks dumped, cleaners run through the tanks. Two days in the shop, two tanks of fuel and a hotel for a night with my sick husband cost $4.155.04.

Had a Dog that Would Not Go the Bathroom

Taking along our fur babies as part of the family while traveling is such as pleasure. It's the easiest way to meet fellow campers while out on the dog walks a few times a day.

Ryan and Kaila couldn't imagine traveling without their dog Bennie. A 10-year-old cocker spaniel, he has always been so well behaved, and house broken since a puppy. We were sure this was going to be an easy transition to the motorhome. Well, it wasn't so easy. On our first trip we couldn't get Bennie to do his business anywhere. He'd hold   it so long even after a walk until we returned to the motorhome where he'd have an accident inside. We were flabbergasted at his defiance. Ryan and Kaila decided, when they returned home, to try a new tactic on the next trip.

As they pulled into their first campground stop day 1, Ryan opted to take Bennie for a walk. With him he carried a bag of gravel from home where Bennie normally did his business. He dropped a small handful on the ground in a dirt area of the park and guess what? You guessed it, Bennie went right to doing his business. I wish I never ....

I wish I never... *had a dog that would not go the bathroom without the smell of where he goes at home.*

Carrying a bag of gravel from his "go" place at home and putting some down every time we need him to do his business. Repairs: $0. Embarrassment cost: Huge!

Drove into a Toll Booth

If you've wanted to go to the Northeastern US, then you had better plan. Planning is what Romana does best. She convinced Mark that seeing the fall colors was must on her bucket list. Studying the color charts from years of fall foliage, Ramona found what was predictably the best two weeks for maximum color change of the fall leaves.

They love their Class C motorhome and have enjoyed over 50,000 miles traveling across America in it. Ramona is the navigator and Mark, stead- fast, is the captain. Traveling from Oregon to the Northeast is at times mundane with fields already harvested, so they tried to stay off the highways and see the small towns along the way.

Excited as they head into Pennsylvania to be seeing the fall colors, they decided they would jump back on the highways up through to the Northeast to avoid difficult traffic and size restrictions. As they pulled up at the toll plaza for the turnpike, Mark pulled just a little too far to the right and as he reached out to hand the money to the toll taker, WHAM! RIP is all they heard! I wish I never....

I wish I never... *drove into the right side of a toll booth with my camper while paying my toll on the other side.*

Ripped off the side mirror, damaging the passenger door.
Repairs: $5,112.00. plus, a toll charge $2.50.

Followed a GPS Without Question

If you've ever used a trip planner tool you know there are lots of "add on" you can explore to send you to restaurants, gas stations, points of interest and more. "Well that's not for us! says Craig. "We just need the basic GPS." Lisa goes along with his stubbornness and they get the least expensive GPS with the basic features. Enter destination, hit GO.

As weekend travelers they saw no need for fancy gadgets. They kept the rig stocked and would just jump in and head out. With an invite in hand, off they went to visit some old high school friends they hadn't seen in 25 years. "Turn right in 2 miles," the GPS would chirp along the way.

As they neared their destination, they started to wonder where exactly their friends lived in this desolate area. Smaller roads led to smaller roads, and then dirt roads without a sign in sight. "You have reached your destination.... Oh no! I wish I never ....

I wish I never... *followed a GPS without question into the middle of a farmer's field that had a resemblance to the movie Deliverance. Taking a 3-point turn and making it into a 30-point turn to get turned around, we nearly buried our motorhome in his field.*

REPAIRS: No repairs, just cost of buying the Truckers Atlas: $55.00 and never blindly following our GPS ever again.

Opened the Refrigerator Door
Right After Driving

If you have ever said, "My idea of camping is the lobby of the Ritz," you may not be alone. The thought of going camping brought back night- mares from Gaby's childhood of bugs, dirt and bad weather. Her husband Jaime had loved camping in a motorhome for years, enjoying the adventures of new places and new experiences.

Persistent on the virtues of camping, Jaime convinced Gaby to rent an RV for a long weekend to prove its will not be roughing it. Packing included favorite bottle of wine and some steaks to demonstrate the great food they would enjoy. "So far so good," thought Gaby, "this might be fun after all."

Pulling into the RV Park all was looking good. Jaime said, "Grab some wine and let's go outside and kick off a little happy hour." Before he could say, watch when you open the refrigerator. I wish I never ....

I wish I never... *whipped open the refrigerator door right when we stopped at camp before realizing the contents may have shifted during the trip.*

Wine and food dumped from the refrigerator breaking glass and flooding the floor of the camper.

REPAIRS: An hour cleaning up the mess; Uber to local grocery to replenish wine and food while dealing with very unhappy wife, will becostly.

Side Swiped a Cement Island
at the Pumps

When you are ready to gas up and go it's the thrill of camping. Mike and Rhonda were excited about their upcoming adventure with months in the planning to sightsee across the western United States. Maps, meals, parks and the like all detailed in their travel plans ready to not miss a thing. They head to the gas station to fill up and begin their grand adventure.

They pull up to the pumps, use the Wise Fuel discount card for the extra 3 cents a gallon discount, and are rightly proud of their frugal ways. Rhonda notes, "We not only saved by coming to the lowest price fuel in town, we saved even more with our discount card. Let's see, that's 50 gallons at a $0.12 per gallon savings at this station and an additional .03 a gallon for our card = $7.50 off!"

Satisfied with their savings they loaded up. As they began to pull out of the station, all they heard was tearing metal, cracking wood and the fresh air coming into their motorhome. I wish I never ....

I wish I never... *pulled the motorhome into a cement island post while pulling out of a low cost, tight fit fuel station.*

Tore the center of the left side of the motorhome open exposing the entire interior. REPAIRS: $12,941.00 less the $7.50 fuel savings for motorhome and thank goodness the station manager was nice enough to say the station damages were minor and he let us leave or shall I say be towed away...

Forgot to Lock the Tool Bay

Who doesn't love having the right tool at the right time when you need it? Ken is an avid Do-it-Yourselfer and while RVing it was no different. He is the guy that sees you struggling with your awning, bad hose fit- ting, or bike needs and jumps into action. He carries the tools you need to fix whatever needs fixing!

When Ken checks his must haves it includes a bay filled with needed tools to fix just about anything while on the road. His tools are a beloved part of his experiences in and out of campgrounds. Packing up to head out for a weekend camping trip includes checking the bay with tools to ensure everything he may need is accounted for.

As he hits the road satisfied with the security of his tools on board he relaxes and begins to think of the fun everyone will have this weekend. As he heads down the last stretch of highway before his exit to the campground, he looks back and screams AUGH! I wish I never ....

I wish I never... *forgot to lock the bay underneath my camper that holds all my tools. The door was bobbing and swinging up and down with the wind. By the time the rig could be pulled to a stop, most all the tools had disappeared.*

Lost nearly every tool in my storage compartment. REPAIRS: $1,472.00 in new tools and fixed open-door latch.

Flooded My Motorhome

The luxury of a washing machine is my favorite thing in my motorhome. Being able to throw in your laundry whenever you feel like it is grand. Not having to sit in a campground's laundry facility, carrying rolls of quarters or having to go buy a laundry card from the office to be able to have clean clothes, is a treasure. Pam loves her washing machine.

After a shopping trip to get a few new pairs of jeans, Pam decided to do the normal wash-before-wearing. Since the jeans were new, she decided the wisest thing to do was use the colorfast sheets designed to keep the dye in the jeans from going everywhere inside the machine.

The washer started like normal and she went to do other tasks. When she came back to check, the A10 fault light was on. What's that? Resets the washer and off it goes again, must be a glitch. Checks back and an- other A10 fault, resets and off it goes. Crazy! Well as Pam went to check on her laundry for the 3rd time to find the A10 fault flashing again, she pulled open the door and whoosh! I wish I never ....

I wish I never... *had to find out that the A10 fault is a washer drain plugged with a colorfast sheet and when opening the door, I flooded blue water across my motorhome.*

Blue dyed water staining my vinyl floors requiring replacement. Towels stained blue, kept for a reminder. REPAIRS: $650.00 for floor replacement.

Hope You are Enjoying the Book

Get one for friends and family

Know someone who's made one of these mistakes? Get a shirt or hat with your favorite - "I wish I never... while RVing" mistake!

Watch for caricature images to be available on Amazon

Had a Tow Bar Break

In the Passing Lane will never mean the same thing again to Oscar. Heading into the 8th year of full time RVing, the rig was in tip top condition. Pride swelled whenever someone asked, "How do you keep your RV in such beautiful condition?" Oscar would reply, "I just try to love her almost as much as my wife."

He and his wife Judi had a strong belief that doing preventative maintenance pays off many times over. Most importantly, they could boast no surprise breakdowns in nearly 8 years.

As they headed towards their winter destination in Arizona, the leaves changing made the ride a spectacular array of beauty up and over the mountains of Southern Colorado. Judi snapped pictures and Oscar just chuckled at how their friends must just hate the play by play of their travels over the years.

Traffic was light at midday as Oscar checked the mirror, and noticed a truck passing them at a high rate of speed down the hill. "Some drivers are just in too big of a hurry," he thought. Funny that truck looks just like mine, and no one is driving it. OH NO! I wish I never ....

I wish I never... *saw my tow vehicle truck passing me going down the mountain at a high rate of speed.*

Tow bar broke releasing truck to speed past us with no one driving. The truck beat us to the bottom of the hill, ending up smashed into a rock wall.

REPAIRS: New tow bar and truck replaced $27,497.00.

Sweltered In 100 Degree Heat

Electrical currents, watts, amps, blah blah blah. Why does there have to be so many pieces and parts when it comes to power? Roberto wasn't big on the handy man type things, so he preferred to buy things with all the bells and whistles ready to go. When he shopped for his new 5th wheel camper, he asked for the works, automatic everything.

He headed from California to his planned weekend visit in Arizona. Thank goodness for the multiple air conditioners on the RV; the summer sun won't feel so bad.

Finally arrived and setting up for the weekend he went to plug in his camper. "What? This plug won't work", bristled Roberto. Now what? I need air. Quick thinking, he pulled out an extension cord and plugged it in. He stretched the cord into the rig and added a multi-outlet. It powered up a couple of fans. No air conditioning! This is crazy. Maybe I can get another space. A quick check at the front desk doused all hope. Sold out! A weekend of suffering endured trying to stay cool with fans in 100-degree temperatures. When only 30-amp service is available, and you have 50 amp needs. I wish I never ....

I wish I never... *found out AFTER a long weekend of using fans in 100-degree heat that all I needed was a simple adapter to convert my 50 amps plug to a 30-amp making it, so I could use my air conditioner.*

Suffered for 3 days running fans to try to cool off. REPAIRS: a near heat stroke, bought a $30.00 adapter to get 50 amps converted to a 30 amp and 20-amp plug. Common sense to ask a neighbor for help would have fixed it.

Left Our Refrigerator Unlocked

Don't you just love a good wholesale warehouse store to stock up for a camping trip? Dylan and Mariah make it a habit to get the bulk food items to make camping easy. They don't plan any grocery trips while camping so that they can maximize their time in the outdoors. Dylan went so far as to get an extra refrigerator to hold more food, so they can last about two weeks, instead of just one, without a trip to a store. On their recent trip, the usual practices filled the inside and outside refrigerator with about a week's worth of food in each of them. Good to go! Nothing but blue skies and clear weather were promised.

When Dylan awoke on their 2nd day, a noise startled him outside the camper. "Oh no!" he yelled, "I forgot to lock the outside refrigerator last night." I wish I never ....

I wish I never... *left our patio refrigerator unlocked and fed the local wildlife a week's worth of food.*

A week's worth of groceries enjoyed by our bear friend. REPAIRS: $75.00 in groceries, a battered refrigerator $225.00 and a trip to the grocery to replace the food. Lastly and most importantly a lesson to never leave it unlocked again.

Locked Myself In the Shower

Girls trip! Not often do we girls get a chance to head out in the RV, but Sue, her daughter and granddaughter were doing just that. A great chance to bond and enjoy time together across three generations. Mariah, the granddaughter is an equestrian with Arabian horses and loves to show them. Sue and her daughter Mandy couldn't be prouder of her. They decided that going together in the RV to the Canadian Nationals competition would be a just reward for all of them.

Night One they stopped late and dry camped in a rest area to maximize their travel time. On Day Two they were headed to a stop about an hour from the horse arena and, while Sue drove, Mandy decided to take a quick shower before arriving. She got into the shower, closed the inside door lock and decided to sit so it was safer to shower. Once wet she was sliding to and fro but finished her shower. As she tried to open the door....oh no! I wish I never ....

I wish I never... locked myself in the shower with slippery hands that couldn't unlock the door. Worse was my mom and daughter were jamming out to the radio and couldn't hear me screaming for help!

Forty minutes sliding around in the shower as we traveled down a country road. Not a smart move. REPAIRS: Can you put a price on dignity? My daughter finally came to tell me we would be there in 15 minutes and rescued me.

Got Hit By a Stupid Driver

Most of us have heard people say the most ridiculous things. Seeing a friend that had hair down their back with a new haircut to their shoulders, they ask, "Did you get a haircut?" My kids call this a Captain Obvious moment.

Lizzy was a long time RVer and had recently bought what she called her "last RV" It was 43' of pure beauty. She had shopped for more than 3 years before making the deal to take her home. She was committed to babying this new coach and ensuring every detail and maintenance was handled timely.

Heading to the dealership for her first checkup and maintenance, Lizzy was a careful and cautious driver, obeying all traffic rules. She exited and stopped on the ramp for the red light, when she heard "WHAM!". I wish I never....

I wish I never... *met the dumbest driver in the world. She exited her vehicle after running into my new 43' motorhome stopped at the traffic light and proclaims, "I didn't see you!" "Really??" was all I could say.*

Heartbroken to have the rear end smashed in on her new baby. RE- PAIRS: $23,539.00 to replace, repair and repaint the entire rear of the motorhome. Luckily no one was hurt. Captain Obvious rides again.

Drove into a Chain Link Fence

Parking with a motorhome can, at times, be a challenge. Over the years, Darrell had proudly put his camper into many tight spots. He would tell people who asked that it is difficult and takes a lot of practice when towing and backing up a motorhome.

On a spring morning, he was headed to the truck stop for propane, a tank dump and fuel fill up. After getting all the services completed he decided to go inside for a few snacks. Like most truck stops it was busy, full of trucks and other RVers. Finding parking can be a challenge, but he spotted an opening he could back into and began the careful line up and then began to reverse.

The spot was tight, and he didn't want his front end to be sticking out so be backed completely up to the chain-link fence behind him. At the last second, he accidentally gives it too much gas and OH NO! I wish I never....

I wish I never... *drove into a chain link fence that had a backhoe bucket parked up against it.*

The shovel tines of the backhoe bucket speared into the rear end of my motorhome leaving 5 large 6" holes. REPAIRS: $9,477.00 body work and paint.

Drove Off With Truck Still in Park

Eddie and Mary Ann were two happy go lucky lovers of the RV life. You'd hear them boast, "Going on 12 years," when asked about their travels. "We have traveled the US, Canada and South America in this baby and are proud to be telling others about it," chimed Eddie as he was packing up his motorhome and truck to head to their next location. "We have everything we need in our motorhome and our truck to do just about anything we want. We pride ourselves on maintenance and safety which has served us well over the years. We have a system to check and double check before heading out and it's saved us a lot of mistakes made by others."

Saying their goodbyes, off they headed around the exit circle when people started yelling, but Eddie and Mary Ann didn't hear them. I wish I

I wish I never... *drove off in the motorhome with the truck in tow STILL IN PARK!*

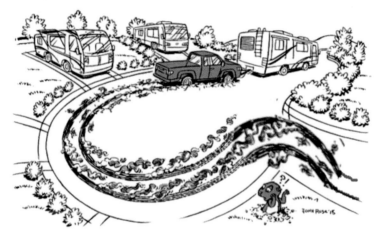

Pulled the truck behind the motorhome through the RV park and tore off the rubber on all 4 tires before being stopped. 44,000 lb. motor- home makes towing even a truck in park a breeze...darn it. REPAIRS: $1,012.00 for tires and alignment.

Left My Dog Alone in the Camper

It's a family affair for many when they hit the road to see the great out- doors. The sign on the Class C reads "Evan, Jodi, Jake & Ike from Austin, TX". We met them on their 1st night and found out that Jake and Ike were their two healer dogs who loved to travel. They were beautiful dogs with lots of energy so went hiking all the time with Evan andJodi.

On Day 2 we decided to try a local restaurant and asked Evan and Jodi to join us. They thought it sounded like fun and the boys, Jake and Ike, yes, the dogs, would be fine for a few hours in the motorhome. So, we all packed up and headed to the restaurant. Great food and great fun was had by all.

As we were pulling back into the camp spots we saw Jake there to greet us. I wish I never ....

I wish I never... *underestimated the power of dogs when left unattended in a camper. Returning to camp to find a new dog door bur- rowed through the entry door.*

New entry door, metal barrier over door interior and crates to keep dogs in when left alone in the camper. REPAIRS: $2,485.00 in repairs & crates purchased.

Left the Stairs Out On The Motorhome

Packing up and heading home is never the fun part of RVing. Leaving new and old friends is only part of the sadness. As Bruce noted, "It's time to pack our stuff and get on the road again." The packing part is the pain in the you know what. Why is it that everything fits so well when you are going camping, but there seems to be no space when you are ready to head back home? We would swear that the stuff expands when we get to a campground. Somehow, we end up getting it all done.

Like most couples, I take the inside and Bruce does the outside stuff. But for a change this time it was just Bruce left to do it all. As he finished the packing and jumped behind the week, he felt pretty good about doing it all by himself. Boy would he show her that he could do it. Until he was at the exit to the campground and heard .... BAM, CRACK, RIP! I wish I never ....

I wish I never... *left the stairs out on our motorhome and sideswiped the exit sign at the RV Campground exit.*

REPAIRS: Replaced steps, paid $250.00 to replace sign, then fixed door damage on RV for $946.23. Embarrassed beyond belief.

Got Sprayed By a Skunk

Safety is something as RVers you get asked about while dry camping (no power, water or sewer hookups) or camping outside a normal camp- ground. Is it safe? Do you worry about burglars? Have you ever had an issue with anyone trying to break in the rig? All good questions.

Lyle and Susan had more than 32 years between them on the open road.

First as semi-truck drivers and then RVers, they have stopped and stayed overnight in many different places. A few weird stories, but mostly al- ways ended up without issues.

On a seemingly quiet night in the small town of Cooke City, Montana, the local store had told them to lock their doors as there had been some recent burglaries. At around 11 PM Lyle heard what sounded like some- one rattling the door of the camper. He let the dog out barking away, grabbed his gun and ran out behind it screaming, "Get out of here!" only to be hit. I wish I never ....

I wish I never... *ran out to scare off a burglar only to find out it was a skunk!*

Getting both the dog and myself sprayed by the skunk. REPAIRS: Sit- ting outside while my wife secured $24 worth of tomato juice for cold outside showers and then sleeping outside for the night to air out. Embarrassment... free.

Dislodged a Bee's Nest

Springtime! Flowers popping up from the previously frozen ground, warmer weather and camping are the happy thoughts. For Hans and Karen from Vancouver, it's the time to get the 5th wheel cleaned up and ready to go. Hans loves the time in the garage tinkering with the latest maintenance to get the rig ready for the road.

Lubricate, adjust, check and clean this and that on the maintenance list are his tasks for today. While under the rig he hears what sounds like a buzzing sound but disregards it. Checks tire pressures, still hears a buzzing sound but can't see anything. Ok, time to do more investigation.

He heads inside to follow the sounds. As he opens the door the sound gets louder. Oh no, there must be bees somewhere. As he opens the overhead compartment.... he screams. I wish I never ....

I wish I never... *opened a cabinet, dislodging a bee's nest and unleashing 100s of bees coming for me! Bee stings on arms and face while running like a maniac out of the garage.*

REPAIRS: Ointment for stings & exterminator to bomb the 5th wheel camper to kill the bees $230.22.

Tried to Park too Close

Only some people are blessed to have and maintain friendships from childhood through retirement. That's exactly what Jake and Jerry pro- fess when they get together. The stories from building go karts and rolling down hills without breaks to high school shenanigans and so on are shared with family and friends.

They have always had a close relationship, said Jake. "But one time with Jerry it went too far." An annual camping to the desert for a month has been a ritual for the two of them and various family would join them for a week or so. The area they go to is on Bureau of Land Management (BLM) land in Arizona. It's open camping with miles of open land as far as you can see. Jake arrived a day early this year and was all set up with no one within a half mile of their camp area.

Jerry looked at the area and decided he wants to camp next to Jake to block the wind. As he was backing up, he heard metal scraping and screeching. I wish I never ....

I wish I never... *tried to park too close next to my "close friend" in the desert! Backed into the slide of my friend's RV Slide.*

REPAIRS: $27,994.04 to replace the slide, paint and repairs. A story to tell forever and never-ending laughs with friends.

Not Turned Off the Grill Inside

"'Go fast, turn left,' is what my wife calls my favorite sport of car racing," says Tim. "But I love it! Since a young boy going to races with my Dad, I've just grown up loving the race track and everything about the people who follow and camp at the tracks for the weekend."

A group of us head to the races every few months to get our racing fix on. It's comradery and competitiveness of who's the best driver, best crew, best cars, etc. We battle each other all weekend long. Win or lose, we love the times together.

Over the years our camping has improved to RVs with all the comforts of grilling, satellite TVs, beverage refrigerators and the likes.

At the end of a race we are rearing to get out of the campground and head for home. Except this time, we might have rushed a little too much. I secured the grill in the trailer and off we went. As I'm driving down the road people are waving me over and pointing frantically towards my trailer I'm towing... A look in the rearview mirror, a quick scream. I wish I never ....

I wish I never... *Put the grill into the trailer without turning it off. Catching my trailer on fire while driving down the highway at 55 mph.*

Totaled the trailer with refrigerator, grill, chairs, TV and all the tailgating gear. Saved the RV. REPAIRS: $17,954.33, replaced trailer and all con- tents.

Forgot to Set the Brake

"Open water and the breeze as we speed along the water is a dream," noted Segrid. "We love our RVing and boating. It is the freedom to enjoy the outdoors.

We had a custom trailer built to hold our boat and a small smart car, so we could get around when we went sightseeing. The motorhome is our tow vehicle for moving, launching and taking out our boat from the water. It took a little while to get used to using our 33' RV as a tow for the boat, but practice makes perfect, so we mastered doing it over time. Well almost.

One day at a busy boat launch we were hurrying to put the boat in. Jeremiah was backing in the boat when another boater cut over onto the dock we were backing into. Jeremiah slammed on the breaks and I went to ask them to move. The man started shouting at me and Jeremiah jumped out to assist. I wish I never ....

I wish I never... *forgot to set the brake before jumping out to support my wife being yelled at by another boater. Looking up I saw the RV and the boat continue to back into the lake.*

The RV was not repairable. Towed to salvage, upgraded car to tow boat from now on. REPAIRS: $237,856.00 the cost of an upgraded new RV as selected by my wife.

Forgot to Put My Tow Car into Park

There is nothing like attending an owners' rally event. The classes, seminars, vendors and camaraderie of other like owners makes it a great investment. A fun-filled week of events in the Midwest with more than 500 others motorhome owners made the trip an exciting adventure. Tyler and Sarah were very excited to be traveling with two friends and their brand-new motorhomes to their first owner rally.

When you arrive, there is a welcome team that greets you with big smiles and directs you to the holding area. So far so good. We made sure they knew we and our friends wanted to follow each other so we could part next to each other at the camp ground. Into the holding area we went following one another to stop and unhook our tow vehicles. More fun people greeting us and giving us the simple directions. Un-hook your vehicles and one of you drive the car and the other the motorhomes. We are so excited! We unhooked the car and Oh no! Oh no! Oh no! I wish I never ....

I wish I never... *forgot to put my tow car into park before disconnecting it from my motorhome. As it rolled slightly down the parking lot into my friends brand new motorhome!*

REPAIRS: Damage to our friends brand new motorhome, $9,439.00. Damage to our tow car, $2.542. Remaining friends... of course.

Forgot to Put Oil Plug Back In

Maintenance on motorhomes is a critical must do. Most say that if you took your normal brick and mortar home down the road at 70 mph it too would take a lot more maintenance. It was time to get an oil change in our old baby "Bitchy" class C motorhome. Checklist looked good from the mechanic, so we were set for the weekend trip to the music festival.

Bitchy is not much to look at but she runs regardless of her squeaks and squawks. Loaded up and headed about an hour down the highway to a weekend festival, she started to have an odd smell as if overheating. It can't be overheating, we just had her in the shop yesterday and all checked out OK. Continuing down the highway, gauges start to go up and down and more smell. Better stop and check it out. We pulled over on the side of Interstate 80 in Nevada and popped the hood. FIRE! I wish I never....

I wish I never... *had a mechanic forget to put the oil plug back into the motorhome engine correctly. Oil dripped onto a hot engine starting a fire on East I-80. Fire extinguisher didn't make a dent in the fire.*

REPAIRS: Volunteer Fire Department arrived in 20 minutes, motorhome was a total loss. Shut down the highway for 1 hour awaiting DOT road review for damage. $7,000.00 insurance payment for the RV (more than I paid for her) plus $500.00 for emergency housing covered tent and accessories for concert weekend camping.

Got Distracted While Back Flushing the Sewer Tank

A little history lesson for you. Old Faithful was named by the Washburn expedition of 1870. They were very impressed by its size and frequency of eruption. Although Old Faithful is not the biggest or even the most regular to erupt geyser in Yellowstone, it is the biggest regularly erupting geyser. The coolest part is it has been erupting the same way for as long as history has recorded eruptions in Yellowstone Park.

Thousands make the trek to Yellowstone National Park each year. Doris and Octavio booked a year in advance for a front row seat to see Old Faithful. A spectacular site. Relaxing after a week in the park Octavio decided to backflush his black tank while Doris went shopping. Everything hooked up, he sat down to wait for the tank to fill up just when Old Faithful erupted. What a sight to see. I wish I never ....

I wish I never... *got distracted while back flushing my sewer black tank. The water built up and shot out the vent pipe with sewage making a brown fountain streaming over the motorhome.*

Old Faithful is amazing, but a fountain resembling it coming out the toilet vent over your camper is not. REPAIRS: Hazmat clean-up, disgusting mess, can't be priced!

Misjudged the Size of the Motorhome

It's amazing that most states do not require any special driver's license to drive a big motorhome off the RV lot. We, like most people, moved up from a trailer to a small motorhome over the years and then finally to our 45' dream machine. Our plans are to travel the Americas over the next 10+ years in luxury, so we put all the bells and whistles on board.

Leroy and Latasha were born and raised in Ohio and loved being snow birds until this last year when they both were officially retired. In Ohio, there are no special requirements for driver's license for RVs, regardless of size. Since they have been RVing for years, they felt comfortable with their new big rig.

Driving down a County road, they noticed flooding and decided to be safe and turn around. A three-point turn is in order and there's no traffic, so this should be easy. I wish I never ....

I wish I never... *misjudged the size of our motorhome while attempting to turn it around on a Country road. We dropped the back-left wheels into a deep ditch, sinking the motorhome to the frame.*

Had to walk about to nearest farm to call for service, no cell service here. Getting a truck large enough to tow us out of the ditch took over 5 hours. REPAIRS: Tow truck costs: $890.00. Repairs to rear storage compartments: $1.829.00.

Disregarded a Local Ranger's Advice

"Give me the sunshine and I'm a happy camper!" proclaimed Patti. "I think I've dragged my poor husband to every beach I can find for the last 4 years of our full-time RVing. He's such a good sport to help me follow the sun. Until one day when I might have pushed ourselves beyond the limits."

Beach camping takes more precaution than camping in your normal concrete pad protected RV Park. Most beach camping allows you to camp near the water's edge on the hard ground or sandy surface. Step- ping out on the sand right from your camper is a special feeling with a million- dollar view of the water. On a recent trip to an Native American Reservation lake in the West, we lobbied for a premier spot on the end of their sandy beach area. "Ok," warns the ranger, "but don't get too close to the water as our winds are mighty strong at times and push the waters up the beach quickly." I wish I never...

I wish I never... *disregarded a local ranger's advice to not park too close to the lake. Winds surprised us, water swelled, and we ended up quickly buried in sand and water.*

REPAIRS: Required an embarrassing call to said "ranger" to admit we were buried and required a tow. Tow truck and many apologies: $572.00. Never say never.

Left Meat In the Freezer

We dread putting our baby away for the winter. Greg and Georgian look forward to the days of retirement and becoming snowbirds so they can use their 5th wheel camper all year long. But for now, it's winterized in November and they get her back out and going in April. After 20 years of RVing the steps to winterize are engrained in them.

On a sunny November day Georgian decided to unload the camper and get the inside ready for winter. Cleaning, removing linens, emptying the pantry and they are all ready. Greg took the steps to winterize the water lines, top off the fluids and several other annual activities. They share in putting the cover on her and reminisceabout this year's fun.

April rolls around and they have their 1st campout planned. They uncover and head inside to start airing it out, repacking it and running water in the lines. As they opened the door all they could do was gasp and gag. I wish I never ....

I wish I never... *left a package of hamburger patties in the freezer all winter long without the refrigerator plugged in.*

REPAIRS: Cleaning all the surfaces in the camper with bleach, many air fresheners and disinfecting the freezer. Lived with a smell for most of the year until giving in and replacing the refrigerator. $1.285.00.

Ignored the High Wind Warning Signs

As we grow up, life gives us many warning signs. There are the do and do not do rules we must follow or there will be consequences. Now some are easy to follow, a few are harder to follow and then there are the ones that might be ok to ignore. Then, as we get older, there are more serious rules like don't enter, no U-turns, one way, speed limits and such that have legal consequences if we choose to not follow them. Being the youngest of eight kids, Daniel was a little bit of a rebel, always the youngest to be picked on, taught all the bad words and certainly how to break rules from his older siblings and how to not get caught. He is one of those people who tries to push the limits on life.

Traveling through Nevada one summer the highway sign flashed, "high winds-high profile vehicles prohibited." Being confident in his driving ability of his motorhome, he pushed on across the valley into a huge win gust. I wish I never ....

I wish I never... *ignored the "high wind warning" signs and flipped over my 30' motorhome on the highway.*

REPAIRS: Luckily no medical injury. The motorhome was totaled by the insurance company and it took 5 hours to turn them back over and tow away. Add to the damages a traffic ticket for unlawful entry in a restricted zone. Total costs, $57,945.00.

Filled Up With Regular Gasoline

"Newbies and Training Wheels," we laughed at the names for people who are just starting out in the RV World. "Well, that's us!" said Cammie. Russ and I have saved for years, read everything we could find on the subject, shopped every brand, until finally pulling the trigger to buy our new 28' motorhome." Like so many others, those first trips are scary, and you try to make sure you follow every checklist you can find to avoid the mistakes of others.

"So far so good," they thought. Three trips and finally feeling more comfortable with how things work. People are nice in the campgrounds and what we didn't remember someone was nice to point out.

We pulled into the fuel station to fill up. Watched pulling into the pump. Not too close to the island posts. All good. Cammie is filling up when I come around the corner to the pump and scream, STOP! I wish I never ....

I wish I never... *mistook a GREEN handle on the pump to mean it's diesel and filled up 100-gallon tank in our motorhome with regular gasoline. Luckily, we realized it BEFORE driving away.*

REPAIRS: Called roadside assistance, waited 4 hours for a tow truck to tow us to the closest diesel service center. Drained tanks, cleaned then had to go refuel $300 in diesel fuel. Total cost: $2,719.00.

Locked Myself Out

Dry camping is when you do not have access to water, sewer or ready power. It's getting closer to nature, farther from the city and you must be reliant on conservation measures to make it all work. Plenty of water in the tanks, solar panels to keep things charged, and planned meals make it easy. The only drawback is if you forget something you are going to do without.

"We like to dry camp about 4 hours from the nearest store." states Julian. "It's truly getting away from it all. The camper is well equipped with everything to suit this type of camping and I've grown to love it."

On a recent trip, Julian realized the one thing he had not planned on. When slamming the door to the camper the latch caught and locked him out. No spare key was stored outside the camper for access. I wish I never ....

I wish I never... *Locked myself out of our camper. Had to break out a window, climb through and sprain my wrist to get in.*

REPAIRS: Broke out living room window, removed glass, climbed through the window and fell to the floor spraining my wrist. Had to go to urgent care, but at least I was able to sleep inside that night. Total cost: $811.75.

Forgot to Lock the Shower Door
Before Traveling

In life we hear people bragging that their such and such is better, bigger, smarter, etc. than your such and such. Well RVers might not always say it, but for some it truly is that they are showing off. Not all of us can afford to be the bigger, better, brighter camper on the block. "Many times, while camping, we bike ride through the park and admire the big rigs, the kayaks, boats, ATV's, big grills, cookers and all the luxuries some people bring along. It's fun to dream, but we always laugh that no one has a bathroom as large as the one in our trailer." says Rocky. "We show it off anytime someone comes over. A large walk-in glass shower is the showcase and beats even the big rigs bathroom accommodations."

On a recent trip, we set up the trailer next to a big rig with all the toys. As we met the owners and shared a beverage, my wife Tina offered to show them our huge bathroom. Entering the bathroom, I heard, "Oh my gosh!" I wish I never ....

I wish I never... *forgot to lock the shower door before traveling. The door had swung open while driving and hit a drawer handle and shattered into a million little pieces that went everywhere! The neighbors did note it was a mighty large bathroom though.*

REPAIRS: Cleaned up all the glass that covered everything in the bath- room. Had to use shower house at campground for the week. Replaced the shower glass enclosure. Total cost: $1,003.00.

Spent 2 Hours Troubleshooting

One of the best things about fellow campers is they are all very helpful when someone is in need. Whether it is something you forgot or a tool you need, there is always someone willing to help.

For Stuart and Michelle, they were glad that their neighbors were so helpful. It was a Sunday and time to pack up and leave for home. Stuart was dumbfounded why he couldn't get his slide to go back in. He tried everything. Several other campers came by to assist. They checked voltages, motors, anything that may be blocking the slide, you name it, to no avail. A group of more than 10 guys had gathered to troubleshoot the problem. With many opinions came many different attempts to get the slide to retract. Nothing seemed to work. It had been two hours of attempts to repair.

Michelle and another wife sat idly by watching when another woman came up to them and asked, "Did you make sure the key is not in the ignition?" I wish I never ....

I wish I never... *spent 2 hours troubleshooting a slide out failure only to have someone ask me I left the key in the ignition. Yep! Fixed it.*

REPAIRS: A hook to hold the keys when we are parked. Embarrassment by myself and all the guys who troubleshot everything except the key in the ignition. $1.95 and never making the same mistake again.

Hazmat at the Truck Stop

We have been Rving for many years and have toted along a large family of 9 children in the process. The kids have grown up watching us do the core mechanical type chores of prepping the rig to head out or head home.

We were about 12 days into a trip and that's about the limit before we have to dump the sewer and refill our water tanks. Ready to fuel, we found a truck stop that had a dump station at the diesel fuel pump set up for RVs. "Now that is handy", said Brett.

As Brett was getting out to fuel his eldest son Josh volunteered to dump the sewer. Now he's seen me do it many times thought Brett, so reassured he can do it off he went to fuel. Josh hooked up the backflow hose and thought all was good, forgetting to pull the dump handle on the sewer. Shortly the sewer was flowing like a fountain out the top and onto Josh. Brett watched from a distance and realized Josh hadn't pulled the release. He yells over, and Josh pulls the handle. Oh NO! I wish I never ....

I wish I never... *watched from a distance as my eldest son attempts to dump our sewer for the first time. Connecting the hose to the backflush on the sewer without pulling the sewer drain handle, a sewage fountain erupted. Then, pulling the handle the hose was not tight and burst off flooding the fuel island.*

REPAIRS: My son was provided a "free shower" by the truck stop. We had to spend 4 hours for hazmat clean up to be performed. The rest of the family sat in horror as the lanes of truckers watched us during the clean-up. No additional charge by the truck stop, but my son has never lived it down.

I WISH I NEVER.... WHILE RVING

& The RV Forget Me Not System

Laugh out loud! This is a book of humor on the mistakes from fellow campers. Whether you travel in a tent, cab over camper, travel trailer, 5th wheel trailer or motorhome you will enjoy this book. It is a group of mistakes made by new and seasoned campers, the results of the mistakes and a hope to save you from repeating them.

This book may be paired with the "RV Forget Me Not System". The system of do not forget tasks is a powerful tool to make sure you don't re- peat the same mistakes. We've tested it with a number of campers and in just 6 months the reviews speak for themselves. Many users coming back to let us know we saved them from making book 2 of "I wish I never .... While RVing".